The Mystery of the Luftha
A Wiseguy Reveals the

by
Robert Sberna
and
Dominick Cicale

The writers thank Ed Scarpo of Cosa Nostra News, Mattie, M.P. and G. for their assistance on this project.

ALSO AVAILABLE...

"House of Horrors: The Shocking True Story of Anthony Sowell" – A true crime account of a serial killer who terrorized women in Cleveland from 2005–2007. Written by Robert Sberna, House of Horrors was named the 2012 True Crime Book of the Year by Foreword Reviews.

"Cosa Nostra News: The Cicale Files, Volume 1: Inside the Last Great Mafia Empire" – a gripping story of mob life (and death) by Ed Scarpo and Dominick Cicale

"Mafia Apocalypse" – a graphic novel written by Dominick Cicale and Robert Sberna, with illustrations by Chris Guiher

LINKS:

www.thecrimebeat.com

www.robertsberna.com

www.cosanostranews.com

www.backdoorentertainmentgroup.com

TABLE OF CONTENTS

INTRODUCTION
By Robert Sberna

While not intended as a biography of Dominick Cicale, this book is based on his experiences as a high-ranking member of the Bonanno crime family. The book also relies heavily on his conversations with people who had firsthand knowledge of the Lufthansa Airlines robbery.

In addition, Robert Sberna has researched the Lufthansa heist extensively and spoken to numerous individuals, including Henry Hill, who had connections to the crime.

Sberna's recorded interviews with Hill were conducted during the summer of 1989 when Hill was living in California. For more information contact Sberna at **robsberna@gmail.com**.

CHAPTER 1
Members Only

It's December 14, 2001 at Rao's, the fabled Italian restaurant in New York's East Harlem. The family-owned institution only has 10 tables—and most are booked nightly with longtime customers.

Iconic New Yorkers Martin Scorsese, Woody Allen, and Al Pacino are regulars, as are musicians, athletes, and high-line figures from the worlds of business and politics.

The titans of the underworld, also, have long favored Rao's. Since its founding in 1896, Rao's has been known for its exclusivity and its wiseguy vibe. On some nights, Rao's can seem more like a Mafia social club than a restaurant. Lucky Luciano, Paul Castellano, John Gotti and Sammy Gravano are among the mob brass who have broken bread in Rao's. Some would even say that its gangland aura is a bigger draw than its legendary lemon chicken or baseball-sized meatballs.

On this night, like most nights, there's a party atmosphere in the small dining room, with diners mingling amongst each other and singing along to the jukebox's Italian crooners and Broadway show tunes.

Three well-dressed, well-groomed men—Vincent Basciano, Anthony Indelicato and Dominick Cicale—are sitting in the midst of the celebration, yet are seemingly apart from it. To some diners, they seem vaguely familiar; perhaps they'd seen their photos in the New York tabloids. Several others cast furtive glances at them, curious about the deferential treatment they're receiving from the waiters and the proprietor.

The men, like nearly all of the other diners, have standing reservations. Each week, they have guaranteed tables to be used by them or their friends and associates. It's been that way since the namesake of their enterprise, Joseph Bonnano, dined at Rao's during his reign from the 1930s to 1960s.

In 2001, the Bonanno crime family, one of New York's five Italian-American Mafia families, was headed by Joe "Big Joey" Massino. The Bonannos had undergone a rocky period during the 1970s and 1980s, most notably because they were infiltrated by FBI agent Joseph Pistone, whose unprecedented undercover work was the subject of the movie "Donnie Brasco."

Pistone's infiltration was so successful that he came close to being formally inducted as a "made" member of the Mafia. After his assignment was terminated, Pistone's subsequent trial testimony decimated the Bonanno leadership. The resulting vacuum sparked deadly infighting among the family's remaining captains (capo or caporegime in Italian).

But with the savvy and cautious Massino at the helm, the family rebounded and was once again a major force in organized crime. The Bonannos even regained their seat on the Mafia Commission, a ruling panel consisting of the heads of the five New York families. Not coincidentally, the rebirth of the Bonanno organization occurred during the rise of Basciano, a relentlessly ambitious capo in the family.

Basciano, a Bronx resident, was famously nicknamed "Vinny Gorgeous" because he owned a beauty salon called "Hello Gorgeous" and for his fastidious grooming, hairstyle and wardrobe. Vinny's growing clout was evidenced by the fact that the Bonnano family's base of power was transitioning to the Bronx from its traditional hub in Brooklyn and Queens.

The Bronx faction had recently received a boost when Vinny affiliated himself with Cicale, who been released from prison two years earlier after serving a 10-year term for drug offenses.

Dominick Cicale, at 32, was 10 years younger than Vinny Basciano. But the two men were remarkably similar in their work ethic, street smarts, and unbridled drive for financial success. In the mob world, making money is the ultimate—if not only—objective. As such, big earners like Dominick and Vinny were the stars of their crime families.

Indelicato, known as "Bruno," was a good businessman, but less driven than the other men. He had spent many years in prison, and was now enjoying his freedom. Bruno was not a go-getter, but he was a legacy— the son of a respected and powerful capo, Alphonse "Sonny Red" Indelicato.

In 1981, Sonny Red, along with two other capos, was lured to a meeting and killed in a power struggle over the leadership of the Bonanno family. Joe Massino, one of the perpetrators of the triple murder, had also intended to kill Bruno. But the younger Indelicato didn't accompany his father to the meeting. Despite Massino's concern that Bruno would try to avenge his father's death—and Bruno's fear that Massino would kill him—the two men maintained a peaceful coexistence.

Now, at Rao's, Vinny, Dominick and Bruno were enjoying dinner while casually discussing business. At some point in the evening, Bruno told Vinny that they should "start putting the money back."

Dominick didn't know what Bruno was referring to, but he didn't ask questions. For the past two years, Dominick had been spending a lot of time with Vinny and Bruno. He'd proven himself a loyal and productive associate. But he wasn't a made member yet, so he understood that he couldn't be taken into full confidence.

"What if Cathy goes in the safety deposit box and sees that all the money is gone?" Bruno asked, his voice tinged with concern.

"You'll get kicked out of the house," said Vinny, laughing. He then added, "How about if we put IOUs in there?"

Bruno half-smiled at the joke. "I don't think we could fit all the IOUs in there."

Dominick was curious. Sensing that it was safe for him to ask—or perhaps he was emboldened by the Remy XO he'd downed—he asked what they were talking about.

Vinny looked at Bruno. With a nearly imperceptible shrug of his shoulders, Bruno signaled his approval.

"Lufthansa," Vinny said.

"The airlines?" Dominick asked.

"That's right," said Vinny.

Unsure what Lufthansa Airlines had to do with their conversation, he asked, "Are you talking about the robbery?"

Vinny nodded affirmatively.

"They never found the money, right?

Again, Vinny nodded. But this time, he smiled. Dominick leaned forward in his chair, anxious to hear what they knew about the Lufthansa heist.

CHAPTER 2
The Heist

     In 1978, when the Lufthansa robbery occurred, Dominick was only 11. But he'd read books and seen movies about the landmark crime—one of the largest cash robberies in U.S. history. And he'd heard stories about the heist while serving time in Allenwood federal prison in the 1990s for a drug conviction. The medium-security facility in Pennsylvania was home to dozens of old wiseguys, including "Mickey Boy" Paradiso, a captain in the Gambino family; Alphonse "Funzi" Sisca; the head of the Gambino's New Jersey crew; Arnold Squitieri, a one-time Gambino underboss; Louie Daidone; former acting boss of the Lucchese family; and Ray Argentina, a Lucchese soldier.

     Sitting in a section of the recreation yard that was the exclusive turf of Italian-Americans, the mob bosses held court, philosophizing and rhapsodizing about the old days with soldiers and associates—men who were affiliated with the mob but weren't officially inducted.

     "We'd all sit together on metal picnic tables," recalled Dominick. "The made guys hanging out with the associates. When you get locked up, your badge (mob rank) gets checked at the front gate. Everyone's equal in jail. The wiseguy hierarchy shit goes out the window. There is rank, of course, but no one pulls it on anyone else. There was a sense of camaraderie among the wiseguys; everyone got the same level of respect."

     The veterans entertained the younger men with their sly braggadocio and one-upmanship, embellishing their roles in notorious crimes, while not directly admitting their participation. When not discreetly taking credit for engineering big scores, the old-timers would offer their critiques of other high-profile robberies, including the Lufthansa job.

     During Dominick's stint in Allentown, he had met Bruno, who was serving time for helping to murder Carmine Galante, the self-appointed acting boss of the Bonnano family. Bruno, during an earlier sentence at the federal penitentiary at Lewisburg, had become smitten with an attractive brunette named Cathy Burke, whom he had met while she was visiting his fellow inmate, John Carneglia.

A member of the Gambino family, Carneglia was a close associate of the family's boss, John Gotti. Carneglia, who was imprisoned for heroin distribution, owned a scrap yard in Brooklyn with his brother, Charles. Federal authorities believe the scrap yard was used for narcotics trafficking, chopping up stolen cars, and disposing of mob murder victims.

According to a New York Daily News article, John Carneglia reportedly used acid to melt the bodies of victims, including John Favara, a neighbor of John Gotti who was marked for death after he accidently drove into Gotti's young son. The article noted that Carneglia liked to remove jewelry from corpses prior to dissolving them and then hang the bling as trophies in his office.

After meeting Cathy Burke, Bruno began corresponding with her. The couple married in 1992, while Bruno was serving time in the federal prison in Terre Haute, Indiana.

Part of their mutual attraction, perhaps, was their underworld pedigree. Like Bruno, Cathy was born into the mob world. Her father was James "Jimmy the Gent" Burke, a Lucchese family associate and the reputed mastermind of the Lufthansa robbery.

Burke was born in 1931 in New York City to Jane Conway, who had migrated from Dublin, Ireland. He never met his father. At age 2, Burke's mother placed him in a foster home. It would be the last time he would see her. His childhood was spent in a series of orphanages and foster homes, where he was neglected and physically abused by staff members as well as his foster fathers and brothers. He took the name Burke from one of the adoptive families who housed him.

Burke's tumultuous and violent childhood seemingly left him predisposed for his outlaw life. In fact, Burke named his two sons Frank James Burke and Jessie James Burke after the infamous gunslinger brothers. Along with Cathy, Burke had another daughter, Robin.

While still in his mid-teens, Jimmy Burke became involved in a wide range of mob-affiliated activities, including extortion, robberies, collecting debts for loan sharks and bookmakers, and murder for hire. While not a member of an organized crime family (in those years, the mob required its members to be 100 percent Italian), Burke was a close associate of Lucchese family capo Paul Vario.

Burke assembled a crew of tough guys and hustlers, including Tommy DeSimone, Angelo Sepe and Henry Hill. Operating out of Queens and Brooklyn, Burke's crew stayed busy hijacking trucks and fencing stolen merchandise.

Burke took a special interest in the street-smart and ambitious Hill, perhaps seeing Henry as a younger version of himself. Burke and Hill also shared a common interest: They were both heavy drug users.

Burke earned his nickname, "Jimmy the Gent," because he was unfailingly polite to the drivers of the trucks he hijacked, often leaving $50 or $100 in their wallets. He would then request that they not divulge his identity to the police. To ensure their cooperation, Burke would take their driver's licenses and warn them that he now had their home addresses.

A tall and physically imposing man, Burke was typically quiet and understated. But he could turn brutally violent in an instant, said Hill. In an interview with author Robert Sberna in June 1989, Hill described the duality of Burke's nature: "Most of the time, he was a big teddy bear. He'd come by my house and bring toys for my kids and actually spend time playing with them. My kids knew him as 'Uncle Jimmy.'"

But even Hill's children were not off-limits to Burke's mercurial temperament. Hill recalled a story that his daughter once told him: "When she was 10, she and I drove to Fort Lauderdale, Florida to meet up with Jimmy at a hotel. My daughter was in the swimming pool, doing handstands and showing off like kids do. She kept yelling at me to watch her, but I wasn't paying attention. So she tried to get Jimmy's attention, but he was ignoring her. So she yelled, 'Hey Jimmy Burke, look at me!'

"According to my daughter, Burke calmly walked toward the edge of the pool and reached down towards her. He put his big paws on either side of her head. Then he lifted her out of the water and said, 'Don't you ever fucking say my name in public again.' He then kissed the top of her head and lowered her back into the water."

Jimmy was everyone's friend unless they made him angry, said Hill. "And then there was no reasoning with him. At that point, you just knew that someone was going to get taken out."

And what made Jimmy angry? According to Hill, money was always a hot button for Burke. He loved making it and hated parting with it. "If he owed someone money, and that person was putting heat on Jimmy to pay, then Jimmy would develop the mindset that the person was trying to take his money from him. And when that happened, there was never a happy ending."

According to Hill, Burke and his crew were responsible for up to 70 murders, with many of the victims stashed in the trunks of abandoned cars in the parking lots of John F. Kennedy International Airport in Queens.

The sprawling JFK was target-rich territory for Burke's crew. Cargo hijackings, drug sales, bookmaking, extortion, theft of parked vehicles, and protection payoffs provided steady income, a portion of which Burke kicked up to the mob bosses who oversaw criminal enterprises at JFK. In the 1970s, the Bonanno, Gambino and Lucchese families all shared the airport action.

While Burke's rackets at JFK were lucrative, they were penny-ante compared to his monumental score on Dec. 11, 1978, when he plundered the cargo room at Lufthansa Airlines for more than $6 million in cash and jewels. In today's dollars, the haul would be worth $23 million.

Lufthansa cargo supervisor Louis Werner set the plot in motion when he tipped off bookmaker Marty Krugman that millions of dollars of untraceable currency was routinely stored in the airport vault after being returned from U.S. military bases and monetary exchanges in West Germany. Werner was reportedly delinquent on gambling debts to Krugman and hoped that the Lufthansa score would settle his tab.

Krugman relayed Werner's information to Henry Hill, who told Burke. Acting quickly, Burke assembled his regular crew, including gunmen Tommy DeSimone and Angelo Sepe, along with several fringe associates and hired hands. Burke enlisted his son, Frank, to drive a "crash car" that would be used to block any pursuing police vehicles.

When his team was in place, Burke reached out to the various mob bosses for approval. Expecting a take of $2 million, Burke reportedly offered the bosses $200,000 to $250,000 each as tribute. Permission was granted and each family sent a representative to look after their interests and take custody of their share. From the Gambinos, John Gotti sent Paolo LiCastri; the Bonnanos assigned Vincent Asaro; and Paul Vario, of the Luccheses, sent his son, Peter.

Guided by Werner's detailed instructions, the crew entered the cargo room without tripping any alarms or alerting airport guards. Ten employees were forced to the floor at gunpoint and handcuffed. A supervisor was ordered to open the vault. The robbers sorted through hundreds of cargo containers until they found the 40 or so bags of currency. They were loaded into a van along with a crate of loose jewels. The entire operation was accomplished in a just over an hour.

The loot was then driven to a garage in Brooklyn, where Jimmy Burke and his son Frank were waiting. After transferring the money and jewels to a sedan, the Burkes drove the vehicle to a safe house to count the haul.

Burke was alarmed when he discovered the amount of money in his possession. Although he increased the Lucchese's share—he gave Paul Vario about $1.2 million—he knew the mob bosses would be concerned that a theft of $6 million was going to bring major heat from local, state and federal law enforcement agencies.

Burke gave shares to some crew members, but only in "dribs and drabs," said Hill. "He gave $10,000 to a couple guys and $25,000 to another. He only paid if he felt that he had to."

Burke's payouts to his accomplices were accompanied by strict warnings to lay low and avoid conspicuous spending.

However, his decision to use amateurs for the robbery would present problems. Burke, who had always zealously guarded his privacy, was now on the verge of becoming accidentally infamous. He became paranoid that his accomplices would become greedy when they learned of the robbery windfall. He was also concerned that the small-time crooks would brag about the robbery or spend their shares on flashy purchases. Burke knew that these unseasoned men couldn't be trusted to keep their mouths shut if they were taken into custody by authorities.

His solution was to eliminate his partners.

CHAPTER 3
Jimmy and Henry

Burke's first victim, Parnell "Stacks" Edwards, was killed by gunmen in Queens. He had angered Burke by not disposing of the getaway van. Rather than following orders and taking the van to a trash compactor, he left it in a no-parking zone on the street, while he smoked pot and took a nap in his girlfriend's apartment. The van, which had had stolen plates as well as Edwards's fingerprints on the steering wheel, was discovered by police.

Accomplice Louis Cafora and his wife, Joanna, went missing in March 1979. Their disappearances occurred shortly after Cafora bought Joanne a pink Cadillac, undoubtedly aggravated Burke, who had warned Cafora to keep a low profile.

Robert McMahon and Joe Manri, who were both employed at JFK airport, were shot to death while sitting in a car in Brooklyn. Paolo LiCastri was also shot to death, with his body dumped in vacant lot in Brooklyn. Since LiCastri, a Gambino soldier, was unlikely to talk about the robbery to authorities, it's thought that he was killed so that Burke didn't have to pay the Gambino organization their cut of the loot. A bold move, but one most likely sanctioned by Paul Vario.

Marty Krugman, who originally brought the robbery idea to Henry Hill, signed his own death warrant when he pestered Burke for the $500,000 share they had agreed upon. When Krugman insinuated that he would inform the feds about the robbery if he wasn't paid, Burke arranged to have Krugman, who owned a wig shop and men's hair salon in Queens, murdered and dismembered at a fence factory owned by Bonanno soldier Vincent Asaro.

Several others who had knowledge of the heist but were not directly involved were also eliminated, including Theresa Ferrara, a goomara of Paul Vario and Tommy DeSimone. When it was learned that Ferrara, a Long Island hairstylist and coke dealer, had met with the FBI, Vario had her killed. Her torso was found floating in a New Jersey river.

Richard Eaton and Tom Monteleone, who were friends of Theresa Ferrara, were murdered after conning Burke out of a chunk of his loot. After learning of Burke's big score, the men convinced him to front $250,000 for a bogus cocaine deal. Monteleone owned the Player's Club restaurant/bar in Fort Lauderdale, a popular mob hangout.

Several heist participants did survive Burke's hit list, including Tommy DeSimone (memorably played by Joe Pesci in "Goodfellas") as well as Angelo Sepe and Frank Burke. DeSimone and Sepe were mob veterans who Burke believed were unlikely to cooperate with authorities if questioned. However, each of the three men would meet their deaths violently, although for reasons unrelated to the heist.

In all, nine people with ties to the case ended up dead. Louis Werner was the only person ever convicted of involvement in the crime. After serving just one year of a 15-year sentence, Werner agreed to become an informant. Several others were placed in the federal witness protection program in exchange for their cooperation. The most notable was Henry Hill, who defected after hearing rumors that Burke was gunning for him.

After entering the witness protection program in May 1980, Hill and his family were relocated to Omaha, Nebraska. The experiences of the Hill family as they tried to acclimate from New York City to Nebraska became the inspiration for Nora Ephron's 1990 film comedy, "My Blue Heaven." (The late Ephron was married to Nick Pileggi, author of "Wiseguy," the bestselling account of Henry Hill's life and the Lufthansa heist.)

While living in Omaha, Hill was flown to New York each week by U.S. Marshals, where he debriefed federal investigators about decades of organized crime activity by Burke and dozens of other mob figures.

Hill's information would eventually help prosecutors link Burke to a Boston College basketball point-shaving scandal that occurred in the late 1970s. Burke was convicted in 1982 for his role in that case, with Hill providing courtroom testimony.

But Hill came very close to missing his court date. In June 1980, one month after Hill turned informant, Burke put out a contract on Hill's life. Burke, at that time, was being held in a federal lockup in Brooklyn on a parole violation charge. The charge stemmed from Burke's association with a known felon, which was Hill himself. Both Burke and Hill had been paroled from prison for the same incident—a 1972 extortion case in Florida in which a friend of theirs had recruited them to beat up a man who refused to pay a debt.

"Burke knew that he was in deep shit when I began cooperating with the government," Hill said. "He knew he had to get rid of me, so he had his attorney relay a message to the street that he was offering up to $100,000 to have me whacked."

Hill said he learned from federal authorities that the contract was picked up by the Westies, a small but feared Irish-American gang operating from the Hell's Kitchen neighborhood on Manhattan's West Side.

In addition to their own rackets of extortion, gambling, protection and drug trafficking, the Westies occasionally performed pieces of work—a gangland euphemism for contract killings—for the Mafia.

"Jimmy had worked with the Westies on several occasions," said Hill. "We all had the Irish thing in common so we got along pretty well. We did some business together."

Despite the measures taken by U.S. Marshals to safeguard Hill's identity and location, the Westies were able to learn where Hill and his family lived in Omaha.

"Truthfully, it wouldn't have been that hard for them find out," Hill said. "I heard that Jimmy Burke even had a crew of investigators out looking for me. The Westies most likely had friends or relatives who worked for the FBI and other federal agencies. They could have bribed or threatened them to get the information. They could have even got it from a corrupt FBI agent or a cop."

In mid-June, one day before two Westies were scheduled to travel to Omaha to carry out the hit, they were drinking in a Hell's Kitchen bar. In the same bar was Wilfred "Willie Boy" Johnson, a mob associate and friend of Gambino boss John Gotti. Half-Native American and half-Italian, Willie Boy stood 6-foot-5 and weighed nearly 300 pounds. Several Mafia families, and occasionally the Westies, employed him as an enforcer.

Noticing Willie Boy in the bar, the Westies invited him over for a drink. Soon, they were spilling their plans to murder Hill.

Willie Boy, however, was a longtime FBI informant. For 16 years, he had lived a treacherous double life. Code-named "Wahoo" by the FBI, Willie Boy continued to work for the mob while giving the feds just enough information to ensure they kept him on the street and turned a blind eye to his criminal activities. When he heard about the Westies' plan, he quickly phoned his FBI case agent.

"That night, I got an urgent call from the marshals who were guarding us," said Hill. "They had us moved out of Omaha within two hours." He recalled that his son's girlfriend came to the house the next morning to pick him up for school. She found the house empty with the front door open. Hill's son was told to never contact her again.

About a week after leaving Omaha, Hill said he learned from federal agents that the Westies—or another set of hit men—had possibly been to Omaha on a surveillance mission.

"There was a park across the street from my house," Hill said. "After some neighbors told police that a couple of suspicious guys were hanging out there one night, the feds investigated. They found cigarette butts and other evidence that led them to believe that my house was being staked out. They also found that two guys connected to the mob in New York had checked into an Omaha motel by using fake identification."

The symmetry of being saved by a fellow informer was not lost on Hill, who said he always liked Willie Boy Johnson.

"I always got along good with him; he liked me fine," Hill said. "Willie Boy was a powerful fucking guy. His nickname was 'Terminator.' He would float around from Burke's crew to Gotti's crew to anyone who could use him as muscle."

Willie Boy's undercover work was costly to the mob, said Hill, noting, "He did a lot of damage during the years he was an informant. Nobody ever suspected him."

Willie Boy's identity was exposed in 1985 by federal prosecutor Diane Giacalone during a public hearing when she was trying to coerce him to testify against John Gotti. Three years later, he was gunned down outside of his Brooklyn home, reportedly as a favor to Gotti.

"Willie Boy was an asshole for staying in New York," Hill said. "He should have got out of there."

With the threat against Hill mitigated, he resumed providing federal prosecutors with damning evidence against Burke. With the Boston College point-shaving case still a couple of years away from being ready to take to trial, Hill was summoned to appear as a prosecution witness at Burke's parole violation hearing.

In July 1980, Hill was taken to a small room in the basement of the Brooklyn corrections center where Burke was being held.

"It would be the first time that I had seen him since I turned informant," said Hill. "Actually, it was the first time that I was confronting anyone associated with the mob."

Hill recalled that he was nervous as the U.S. Marshals escorted him into the room. "It was pretty crowded in there," he said. "Ed McDonald, the U.S. Attorney was in there with some other feds. Jimmy Burke was with his attorney, Michael Corio. When I walked in, Jimmy was wearing a prison jump suit, sitting down. He looked over at me and I could tell that he had fear in his eyes. He looked upset and worried."

Burke wasn't particularly worried about Hill's testimony in the parole violation case. "He would only get a couple of years in prison for that," Hill said. "He could do that time standing on his head. He was worried about the other cases I was helping the government develop—the Boston College point-shaving and the murders I knew about."

As the parole violation hearing progressed, Burke's facial expression turned from fear to disgust, said Hill.

"I don't think he was angry at me," said Hill, explaining, "I think he was disappointed that I had beaten him to the punch. He was mad at himself that he didn't whack me before I flipped. Now, with me helping the government, Jimmy knew that he was going to get sent away for a very long time."

Even with Hill's cooperation, the feds failed to directly implicate Burke in the Lufthansa case. But Hill's testimony helped convict him of the murder of Richard Eaton, the drug dealer who had hustled Burke out of $250,000.

Incensed that Eaton had ripped him off, Burke tortured and strangled him. He left Eaton's hog-tied body inside of a rusted truck trailer in Brooklyn, where a group of children discovered him. Burke was connected to the grisly murder when investigators discovered an address book inserted into the lining of Eaton's jacket that contained Burke's phone number and address.

Hill's corroborating testimony cemented the case for prosecutors. "Burke told me that he had killed Eaton," recalled Hill. "He said, 'I whacked the fucking swindling cocksucker.' Jimmy wasn't even worried about the $250,000. He said he would go after Eaton's partners for the money."

Burke, whose lust for money was legendary, seemed more interested in avenging his wounded pride than recouping his financial loss. The soured drug deal with Eaton was a rare misstep for the business-savvy Burke, who was earning close to $1 million a year dealing heroin, said Hill.

Hill estimated that Burke's net worth was close to $6 million, including his cut of the Lufthansa loot, which he believed was about $4 million. Although Hill broke off contact with Burke too soon after the Lufthansa heist to know where the loot went, he said it was plausible that Jimmy had stashed it.

"I know that he used some of it to finance big drug deals, but he was too secretive to let anyone know where he put the rest of the cash," said Hill.

In 1985, Burke was given a life sentence for the Eaton murder.

When Hill was asked how he felt about helping to lock away Burke, whom he had met in 1956 when he was a 13-year-old gofer for neighborhood wiseguys, Hill was philosophical.

"If it wasn't me, it would have been someone else," he said. "We're all living on borrowed time in this life. Jimmy knew that. He probably figured I was doing what I had to do to survive. After Jimmy got convicted on the Boston College thing, somebody asked him what he thought about me testifying against him. He said, 'I guess Henry loved his family more than he loved me.'"

Jimmy Burke was rather unique in gangland for his earning power and his longevity. He was a ruthless, yet cunning, politician who maintained his independence while forging alliances with mob shot callers.

But even the Jimmy Burkes are replaceable, said Hill. "Whenever there's money to be made, there will always be smart people who are willing to cheat, steal and kill for it," he said. "There will always be Jimmy Burkes and there will always be the mob."

Burke was incarcerated in Wende Correctional Facility in Buffalo, New York. After serving 11 years of his sentence, Burke was diagnosed with lung cancer. He died on April 13, 1996 at age 64.

Henry Hill died in 2012 in Los Angeles, the day after his 69th birthday.

CHAPTER 4
"A Nice Score"

Dominick Cicale didn't personally know Henry Hill or Jimmy Burke, but he was close to Burke's associates and family members. When asked about Burke, Dominick didn't mince words, saying he was a stone-cold killer, a drug addict, an alcoholic, and a compulsive gambler.

"However, all of that goes hand-in-hand with the life," he added. "When you're living the fast life like Jimmy Burke was, you're out there all the time. You're going to be gambling and hitting the after-hours joints; it's all part of it."

Calling the Lufthansa robbery a "nice score," Dominick said, "It was a nice payday for Jimmy Burke. But not for the guys he killed, of course. Burke had used street guys for the heist. He realized that these guys were a risk to cooperate with law enforcement and give up the gang. He couldn't trust them when the heat came down—they weren't tough guys. But in a way, it was a smart move on his part to use accomplices who weren't made guys. Burke knew he wouldn't have been able to get away with killing anyone of serious stature. His master plan may very well have been to get all those suckers involved and then kill them at the end of the job. It was naïve for the JFK airport employees to think they could do business with the mob. They became blinded by the glamour and the idea that they were going to make a lot of money. Jimmy would play on their greed and entice them. They felt secure with him because of his connections to Paul Vario and the Lucchese family. They felt no one could screw them over. But all along, Jimmy was fucking them over."

Dominick said that Burke most likely had free reign to eliminate anyone, as long it wasn't someone of stature. "He'd tell Vario, 'We can't trust this guy,' and Vario would go along with it. Burke and Vario had a mutually beneficial relationship. Vario needed Burke because he could do stuff off the record. Since Jimmy Burke was a freelancer and didn't have a pact with anyone, Vario could use him to kill someone in the Lucchese family, whenever that was necessary. It was less conspicuous and less awkward to use Burke than having another family member do it."

With Paul Vario backing Burke's criminal activities—and Burke kicking fat envelopes to Vario—the two men had a profitable partnership for many years. Dominick said that Burke certainly had enemies; men who were jealous of his success or resented him because he was so close to Vario. But they knew that they would have to deal with Vario if they went after Jimmy the Gent.

"And all Jimmy had to do was take care of Paul," Dominick said. "As long as he sent him money, he was good. And then it was up to Vario to kick the money up and over to the other bosses, if that was necessary. It's very competitive in the mob world. Everyone wants to be close to the bosses. But in this life, money talks and bullshit walks. At Christmastime, the gifts would roll in for the top guys. We're talking big numbers. One year, I gave $300,000 to Joe Massino and Vinny. If a boss has 15 or 20 capos in his family, it really adds up. Joe Massino had a stockpile of $7 million in gold coins and cash. He hid money in his house and the homes of his relatives. At a certain point, it becomes hard to launder that much money each year. You try to wash your cash through your businesses a little bit at a time. Bars and strip clubs are popular places to launder money, as well as parking garages, valet companies, and car washes."

Because Burke was a big earner, his drug habits were tolerated. But small players who had drug and alcohol issues, such as Henry Hill, weren't regarded so charitably.

"When I was running a crew, I might put up with a guy who had issues if he was an earner, but there weren't a lot of drug addicts that I could trust," Dominick said. "Hill was around killers so he got his reputation from them. He was on the coattails of people who had balls. But I don't think Paul Vario would have given him the time of day. It was Jimmy Burke who had the respect. Jimmy needed someone like Henry to pick up his drugs for him and drive him around."

When Jimmy Burke died, many of the secrets of the Lufthansa heist went to his grave with him—including the whereabouts of the loot. Police only found a small amount of the cash in circulation. Burke presumably laundered some of his estimated $4 million take through mob-affiliated bars and businesses in order to yield income that he could legitimately spend. But in the years since the robbery, law enforcement authorities and journalists have been mystified that millions of dollars seemingly disappeared. Authorities have also been unable to find the jewels taken from the JFK vault. It's unlikely that $1 million in jewels could have been fenced without attracting attention.

Burke was known as a spendthrift—he lived in a modest neighborhood in Queens and preferred to save his money. Associates of Burke's say he had a strong interest in ensuring that his family was financially secure, especially his daughters, Cathy and Robin. Perhaps his attentiveness to their security stemmed from the chaotic, unsettled nature of his own childhood.

In a bitter irony, the Lufthansa heist, which was far more lucrative than Burke could have imagined, was also the beginning of the end of his very successful criminal career. He spent increasing amounts of time engineering the elimination of anyone who could link him to the crime. He also was paranoid about spending the money. Burke knew that any large purchases would attract attention from law enforcement or even mob bosses who believed they were entitled to a cut of the proceeds. Burke reportedly gave up on attempts to launder the money, deciding that transforming the Lufthansa millions into spendable cash was cumbersome and risky. So, he decided to stash his money.

CHAPTER 5
Ferretina

In Rao's Restaurant, 23 years after the Lufthansa Airlines robbery, Vinny Basciano and Bruno Indelicato trickled out details of the Lufthansa robbery and the whereabouts of the loot. The two caporegimes seemed undecided whether they wanted to brag about their inside knowledge to Dominick or protect their secrets.

Dominick could only wait patiently as the story teased out. His thoughts drifted back to a night two years earlier, in the same restaurant, when he had first met Vinny. He was introduced by Bruno, his former prison buddy. During his stretch in federal lockup, Dominick had come to admire the loyalty, brotherhood and respect shared by the mob guys. When a made guy arrived in prison, they were taken care of by their associates on the outside. Not only were they sent money and clothing, but their wives were provided with financial assistance. That familial bond appealed to Dominick, who was raised by a free-spirited mother and had little contact with his father.

When Dominick left prison in 1999, he arranged for Bruno to set up a meeting with Vinny. The sit-down was approved and Dominick arrived with his godfather Peter Cicale, a Lucchese mob associate who had played a character named "Pete the Killer" in "Goodfellas."

During their initial conversation, Vinny had peppered Dominick with questions, evaluating his ambition and character and getting a sense for his loyalty and discretion. Vinny was impressed by Dominick's poise, his rugged physique, and his machismo. He quickly gained Vinny's trust and approval. Over the past two years, Dominick had proven himself a good earner who could also be counted on to use muscle when necessary. Now, Vinny and Bruno were bringing Dominick into their confidence, a clear signal the men were grooming him for a greater role in family business.

Leaning closer to hear the two capos' voices amidst the chatter of conversation and the jukebox in Rao's, Dominick listened as Vinny explained that Jimmy Burke had asked a friend to rent a safety deposit box at a bank in Queens. Burke then placed between $2 million and $4 million in the box. He gave the keys to the box to his two daughters. Burke was known to have a close relationship with his girls, particularly Cathy.

Vinny told Dominick that the Burke sisters were aware that the safety deposit box contained a large amount of cash, but it's not certain how much of the money they may have spent. Like their father, both women lived modestly and were hard workers. Robin drove a school bus in Queens and Cathy owned a Manhattan jewelry store, so perhaps the women were saving the money as a rainy day fund or a retirement nest egg.

Their brother, Jessie James Burke, had been educated in private schools and was an attorney on Long Island, specializing in real estate law. Their other brother, Frank, had been shot to death in Brooklyn in 1987 after an altercation in a bar.

If, in fact, Cathy and Robin were counting on their father's stash to fund their retirement, they were facing a major disappointment. By 2001, the box had been emptied.

Dominick listened, with equal parts amusement and surprise, as Vinny explained that he and Bruno had convinced Robin Burke to turn over her key to the box.

"Bruno knew about the money through Cathy, his wife," said Dominick, recounting Vinny's story. "In those days, Cathy was basically in control of everything—the safety deposit box, her mother Mickey, and the rest of the family's affairs. She would have never given Vinny and Bruno access to the box. Even though she was married to Bruno, she had an independent streak. She had her jewelry business, she traveled to Paris several times a year, and she even owned rental property that Bruno didn't know about. Cathy was a smart girl. She acted tough, but she was very nice. I got to know her well through Bruno. She came to my daughter's christening and I went to her daughter's birthday parties."

Cathy, perhaps more than her other siblings, was endowed with her father's forceful personality. Henry Hill recalled a family trip that he, Jimmy Burke, and their daughters had once taken. They had stopped at a restaurant and Hill and Burke argued over the check, with each insisting on paying. Cathy, at age 9 or so, pulled the check from her father's hand and said, "Dad, let Henry pay the check. It will make him feel like a big man."

Along with inheriting her father's strong will, Cathy also was the heir to his real estate. She took possession of a house in Queens that came with a gruesome secret. In June 2013, the FBI, acting on a tip, dug around and in the home as they searched for traces of Paul Katz, an associate of Jimmy Burke's who disappeared in 1969.

Investigators discovered bones buried in the ground that were determined to be human. DNA tests confirmed they were indeed a match for Katz, who once owned a warehouse that was used by mob figures to store stolen goods. When the warehouse was raided, Burke and Vincent Asaro suspected that Katz was an informant.

On the night of his death, Dec. 6, 1969, Katz left home after receiving a phone call. He told his wife that he was going to "meet the guys at the candy store."

Katz's wife, perhaps sensing danger, begged him not to leave. Katz assured her that he would be back soon. He walked out of the house, saying goodbye to his five children, who were watching television in the living room.

Authorities say that Burke beat and strangled Katz with a dog chain. He then buried Katz's body under the basement floor of the Queens house that eventually became the property of Cathy Burke.

In late 1998, when Bruno first told Vinny about the safety deposit box containing the Lufthansa cash, Vinny came up with the idea to approach Robin with a scheme, while keeping it a secret from Cathy.

"Robin was not a dummy," said Dominick. "But she was more trusting of Vinny and Bruno, who was her brother-in-law. So they told Robin that they needed to borrow money for a business deal they were arranging. They asked her to not tell Cathy about the loan, and they promised to return the money quickly with interest. They basically charmed Robin into giving them the money."

From 1999 to 2000, Vinny and Bruno made several trips to the safety deposit box, taking out $200,000 to $500,000 at a time.

A portion of the money did go towards a business deal, of sorts. Vinnie was eager to invest in an animated movie about ferrets, tentatively called "Ferretina." The project was brought to Vinny's attention by Frank Avianca, a producer of horror movies and the occasional porn flick.

Before entering the movie business, Avianca had a singing career under the name Frankie Sardo. In February 1959, he was part of the Winter Dance Party tour with Buddy Holly, Richie Valens and J.P. "The Big Bopper" Richardson. On February 2, after a concert in Clear Lake, Iowa, Sardo traveled to the next venue by bus with Waylon Jennings and Dion and the Belmonts, while the headliners took a plane. In a tragedy dubbed "The Day the Music Died," the plane crashed in a cornfield, killing Holly, Valens and Richardson.

In preparation for producing "Ferretina," Frank Avianca thoroughly researched ferrets, said Dominick. "He found out that ferrets were the second-most popular domesticated animal in the U.S. His statistics showed that nearly 20 million people owned ferrets, so the demographics were good. The movie was going to be a love story about ferrets that came from Europe to America. The ferrets get separated, go through some struggles, and then find each other again."

Vinny gave Avianca upwards of $250,000 for the film project. Although legendary actress Chita Rivera reportedly agreed to star in the movie and Sony Pictures had committed $20 million towards marketing, "Ferretina" never went into production. ("It's too bad it wasn't made," said Dominick. "I was promised a 10 percent cut from Vinny's end.")

And what happened to the rest of the Lufthansa money? Dominick was stunned to hear that Vinny had blown it all at casinos.

CHAPTER 6
The "System"

The first batch of money taken from the Burke's safety deposit box totaled about $500,000. Vinny promptly lost it all betting sports games and playing blackjack at Foxwoods Resort Casino in Connecticut.

"I guess I shouldn't have been surprised," said Dominick. "When I got to know Vinny, I realized that he was a degenerate gambler. He had been banned from all the casinos in Atlantic City because he didn't pay his debts. He used the money from the safety deposit box to pay off his losses and to be able to keep gambling."

Dominick had been with Vinny on numerous occasions when he lost thousands of dollars—even hundreds of thousands of dollars—playing blackjack.

"He thought he had a system," said Dominick. "A compulsive gambler always thinks he has a system. They always think they can beat the house. But Vinny's system didn't make sense. If he won, he'd leave his money down. But he'd also chase his losses. His system was always changing. He had no discipline. And when he first approached a table, he'd try to get the casino to raise the limit to the maximum, at least $2500 or even $5000 a hand. He was trying to scare the amateurs off the table. If anyone stayed, he figured they knew what they were doing. Sometimes, he'd play two chairs or even three chairs at a time."

Quitting was never an option for Vinny, said Dominick. "You couldn't convince him to leave the table. It was like telling a junkie he couldn't have heroin. Vinny wouldn't step away until there was no money in his pocket…or mine."

Since Dominick owned legitimate businesses, including a profitable mortgage company and an auto body repair shop, the casinos granted him credit lines of $300,000 or more.

"When Vinny went broke, he would tell me to tap my credit line. I couldn't say no—he was my friend. So I'd give him the money and then tell me we'd go half on any winnings. There rarely were any. At least I got a lot of comps from the casino, since the credit lines were all in my name. Vinny ended up owing me $1.1 million that I never recouped."

Vinny was able to maintain his cool while gambling, despite his reputation for having an explosive temperament. He was aware of his temper and even joked about it, said Dominick, explaining, "When his anger was building, Vinny would say that his count would go '1, 2, 60,' and then it was action time. It seemed impulsive, but it showed the severity of Vinny and his crew. He would try to end threats quickly before they started. It sent a message that we didn't mess around. People knew that we would rock-and-roll."

In the casinos, however, even while facing immense losses, he was stoic. "The only time I ever saw him get mad at a casino was at Foxwoods when he thought a pit boss was giving him nasty looks. Vinny was down about $75,000. He looked at the pit boss and said, 'Let me ask you something: Why the fuck are you looking at me like that?' The pit boss denied that he was looking at him. So Vinny said, 'You're not even smiling. Get that nasty look off your face. I should be the one looking nasty; I'm down all this money.'"

Dominick recalled that the only person who could pull Vinny away from the blackjack tables was his wife, Angela. "He wouldn't listen to me, but he didn't want to seem like a degenerate gambler in front of his wife. So he'd call it a night when she told him to."

Nevertheless, Dominick was somewhat surprised that Vinny had needed to tap into Cathy and Robin Burke's safety deposit box. Dominick estimated that Vinny was earning $500,000 to $1 million a year just on his bookmaking and the many illegal Joker Poker slot machines that he controlled in New York bars and social clubs.

Vinny's net worth in the early 2000s was about $11 million, according to federal authorities who developed several racketeering cases against him, including murder.

Noting Vinny's significant earnings, Dominick said that his one-time mentor's income included about $200,000 in tribute payments from Bonanno crew members each Christmas. "But as fast as the money came in, Vinny spent it on gambling binges," he said.

Dominick, only a casual gambler himself, said that Vinny was embarrassed by his gambling problem, but couldn't stop himself.

"John Gotti was the same way," Dominick said. "He and Vinny would blow $200,000 to $300,000 on a weekend betting football. They were always behind the dollar. Vinny did try to pay down his debts. He ended up paying off about $900,000. But he always needed more money to gamble. He spent so much money in Las Vegas that the casinos would send a Learjet to pick him up. They would put him up in the Elvis Presley suite [at the former Las Vegas Hilton]. Vinny would joke that the casinos would fly him to Vegas and then to one of their sister casinos in Biloxi, Mississippi for a steak dinner, and then back to Vegas for more gambling. In total, he ended up losing about $16 million to the casinos."

Not only did Vinny lose all of the Lufthansa money, but he also took $40,000 from the safety deposit box that had been earmarked for college tuition for Robin Burke's daughter. The money had been given to Robin by Ciro Perrone, a powerful capo in the Genovese family. Perrone's son, Frank, was the father of Robin's daughter.

Although Robin was assured that her daughter's college money would be returned, the "loan" was never repaid. When asked if Vinny and Bruno feared retribution from Ciro Perrone, Dominick said, "Ciro would have been upset that they took his granddaughter's money, but what could he do? Vinny and Bruno were killers in their own right. At the end of the day, they could tell Ciro that Robin gave the money to them. It was none of his fucking concern."

To Cathy Burke, however, the missing money was a major issue. She discovered the box was empty in 2004. "She was furious," Dominick said. "She was so angry at Bruno for taking the money that she nearly ended her marriage to him."

CHAPTER 7
Victims and Victors

Bruno Indelicato, it seemed, was also a casualty of Vinny's gambling problem. Bruno had neither a drug nor a gambling problem, and he hadn't particularly wanted to pilfer the Lufthansa loot. He was just looking for some spending money. He believed that Vinny would return the money to the safety deposit box, or he wouldn't have gone along with the scheme, noted Dominick.

"Bruno was easily influenced," Dominick said. "He wasn't particularly sure of himself. If you told him something, he'd listen. But he didn't have an air of confidence. He was comical and entertaining; basically a 50-year-old acting like a 20-year-old."

Bruno had been in prison from 1986 to 1998, sentenced for killing Carmine Galante. In Dominick's view, Bruno's long stretch in prison had institutionalized him. He had a no-show job at a mob-connected trucking company, where he hoarded numerous cans of tuna fish and bottled water in his office, just as he had in prison. The job paid Bruno $50,000 a year on the books, with another $5,000 a month in unreported cash. Bruno spent about two hours a day at the trucking company, then went home to take a nap and exercise, according to Dominick. He added that the cushy job was given to Bruno out of respect for his late father, Sonny Red Indelicato.

The Mafia world, along with its inherent treachery and constant life-or-death proposition, is rife with irony. When Bruno killed Galante, he created a leadership void that would lead to the murder of his own father.

Galante, who had strong-armed control of the Bonanno family from the incarcerated Philip Rastelli, operated a very lucrative heroin distribution network. The other four New York families were angered that Galante refused to share his enormous heroin-dealing profits, so they approached the Mafia Commission for permission to eliminate him. The hit was quickly sanctioned.On July 12, 1979, Bruno, along with Dominick "Sonny Black" Napolitano and Dominick Trinchera, opened fire with handguns and shotguns on Galante as he ate lunch in the outdoor garden of the Joe and Mary Italian-American Restaurant in Bushwick, Brooklyn. Killed with Galante were Leonard Coppola, a Bonanno capo; and Giuseppe Turano, the restaurant's owner who was also a Bonanno soldier. As a reward for killing Galante, Bruno was promoted to capo.

Galante's murder sparked a power struggle among two factions in the Bonanno family. Capos Sonny Black Napolitano and Joseph Massino supported Rastelli as the next boss, while another faction that included capos Sonny Red Indelicato, Philip Giaccone and Dominick Trinchera wanted to assume power for themselves.

Massino, however, petitioned and received the go-ahead from the Mafia Commission to whack the opposing capi.

Indelicato, Giaccone and Trinchera were lured to a meeting and then executed in a building owned by Salvatore "Sammy the Bull" Gravano, the Gambino underboss. Bruno had planned to attend, but Sonny Red reportedly called him off, fearing that there would be bloodshed. Instead, Sonny Red asked Frank Lino to drive him to the meeting. However, Sonny Red told Bruno that if he didn't return, Bruno should kill the rival capos. During the massacre of the three men, Lino escaped unscathed by running out the door.

With Sonny Red dead, the Bonanno family feared that Bruno would seek vengeance. As a preemptive measure, Sonny Black Napolitano ordered FBI infiltrator Joseph Pistone (known as Donnie Brasco to his duped mob colleagues) to clip Bruno, but the hit was cancelled. Sonny Black had promised Pistone that he would get "straightened out" (inducted into the Mafia) if he succeeded in killing Bruno.

When Bruno left prison in 1998 and moved home to Cathy Burke in Howard Beach, Queens, he negotiated a truce with Joseph Massino and took over his father's old crew.

While Dominick Cicale said he had a close relationship with Bruno, he also questions his honor and self-respect. "Bruno knew that Joe Massino was behind the death of his father, but he allowed himself to be in a state of denial to save face about it. Bruno was told by John Gotti that Massino had nothing to do with Sonny Red's death. That was a lie. Gotti knew that he could control Massino if he was boss of the Bonannos, but he knew that he couldn't control Sonny Red and the other capos, so of course Gotti was all for their murders."

Dominick said he also questions why Bruno didn't back up his father when he was summoned to the fatal meeting. "I don't know why Sonny Red went to that meeting without realizing that he was going to get killed. In this life, some guys get false beliefs about their own mortality. Maybe Sonny Red thought he could talk his way out of trouble. But if I was Bruno and my father didn't come out of that meeting, I would have waited for the shooters to come out and I would have picked them off. Or I would have gone in with two pistols and shot it out. At least I would have gone down with my head held high."

In yet another irony, although Bruno wasn't there for his father when he needed backup (in Dominick's view), he often showed concern for his father-in-law, Jimmy Burke. Bruno would lament that Burke was going to spend the rest of his life in prison.

"We'd tell him, 'Don't worry, you're married to his daughter. You'll be spending his money,'" Dominick said.

But the last of Jimmy Burke's money is gone, essentially thrown away by Vinny Basciano. In a poetic turn, the mob careers of Basciano and other high-ranking Bonannos are also spent. A family that had fought back from the brink of extinction had now turned on itself, with even its own boss, Joe Massino, wearing a wire. The Bonanno family, which traces its 120-year history to the town of Castellammare del Golfo in Sicily, had prided itself on being the only New York Mafia family to never have one of its made men turn informant.

In the book "Sixth Family," authors Lee Lamothe and Adrian Humphries wrote:

Even those gangsters who faced certain death from their colleagues for vouching for Donnie Brasco refused to cooperate, despite overt offers from the government. Sonny Black Napolitano refused to accept even an FBI agent's telephone number. Instead, he handed his jewelry to the bartender at the Motion Lounge social club, said he might not be coming back and glumly went to meet mob colleagues who, as he suspected, had orders to kill him. On orders from Gerlando Sciascia and Joe Massino, Frank Lino lured Sonny Black to a meeting at a fellow mobster's house and then pushed him down a flight of stairs. At the bottom, he was shot, but the gunman's weapon jammed. As he lay on the floor wounded, Sonny Black looked up at his friends and implored them, "Hit me one more time; make it good." They complied.

Sonny Black's body was found with his hands chopped off to signify that he had shaken hands with Donnie Brasco, an FBI agent.

But in 2002, ex-capo Frank Coppa became the first made member of the Bonanno family to cooperate with the government. Once Coppa turned, others followed. First, Sal Vitale, the family's underboss turned state's witness; and then Frank Lino. In 2004, federal prosecutors landed a whale: Joe Massino decided to cooperate rather than face a death sentence after being convicted of murder. Massino was the first boss of an organized crime family to break omerta, the blood oath of silence.

In 2006, Dominick was arrested after Vinny spoke indiscreetly about him to Massino, who was wearing a wire. At that point, Dominick was a capo overseeing a crew of 26 men. He had amassed more than $10 million, much of it through legitimate construction and real estate businesses. But after his arrest, he came to realize that loyalty and honor were merely pretenses feigned by Massino and the other old-timers. So he cut a deal. He implicated Vinny and Bruno in the 2001 shooting death of Bronx junkie Frank Santoro, who had reportedly threatened to kidnap one of Vinny's sons.

In 2007, Vinny was found guilty of the Santoro murder. In 2011, he was also found guilty of ordering the 2004 killing of Randy Pizzolo, a small-time Bonanno associate who had angered Vinny because he "had a big mouth."

Even as he faced the possibility of death sentences during his 2007 and 2011 trials, Vinny maintained his carefully coiffed and dressed persona. He was granted approval by the judge to have access to five of his tailor-made suits, one for each day of the week. Vinny also made headlines when he got the judge to agree to allow his ex-wife Angela and his mistress Deborah Kalb to visit him on alternating weeks while he was awaiting trial in 2011.

Vinny is now serving two life sentences at the federal "supermax" prison in Florence, Colorado. Known colloquially as the ADX (Administrative Maximum Facility), the institution is the highest-security prison in the U.S.

Designed for the worst of the worst, Vinny's fellow inmates include the "Unabomber" Ted Kaczynski, 1993 World Trade Center bombing mastermind Ramzi Yousef, Oklahoma City bomber Terry Nichols, and 9/11 conspirator Zacarias Moussaoui. Not that Vinny sees much of his neighbors—inmates at the ADX are locked up 23 hours a day in solitary confinement.

Vinny, who had lived with his wife and children in a stately, columned home in Scarsdale, an affluent New York City suburb, now spends his days in a 12-by-7-foot cell with solid metal doors and a single window that is only four inches wide. He sleeps on a thin mattress atop a concrete slab.

For several hours a week, he's escorted with a group of other prisoners to an outdoor recreation area, where each prisoner is confined to an individual cage. Vinny also has the option of exercising privately in an indoor windowless room that is equipped only with a chin-up bar. At mealtime, there are no trips to a cafeteria—food trays are slipped through a slit in his cell door.

Vinny's confinement to the ultra high-security prison is due, in large part, because he had been accused of ordering "hits" on the judge, prosecutor and several cooperating witnesses during his trial in 2007. Now, because he has no contact with other inmates and is allowed no visitors, authorities believe they have minimized the risk of Vinny passing orders to associates on the outside.

Despite the stark reality of spending the rest of his life in the supermax, it's not likely that Basciano, 55, will ever cooperate with the federal government, said Dominick.

"He has deep roots in the Bronx and his sons are in the street," he said. "They would endure a lot of shame if their dad became a turncoat. They would have to be uprooted and moved."

Vinny Basciano, at one time, the acting boss of the Bonanno family, will most likely never see the Bronx again. And now, it seems that his three sons have embraced the family business. The Basciano brothers—Vincent Jr., Stephen and Joseph—pleaded guilty in 2014 to federal marijuana trafficking charges.

The brothers were part of a drug ring that distributed thousands of pounds of weed in New York from 2009 to 2013. Dominick, who knew all three brothers, expressed disappointment that Joseph, 28, had been caught up in the criminal life. "He's a good young man," he said.

Stephen Basciano, however, had long seemed destined for prison, said Dominick, noting, "He's a career criminal who has sold drugs and committed various crimes since 2002. Of the three brothers, he's the most dangerous, due to his impulsiveness. Basically, he acts without thinking."

At his sentencing, Stephen, 31, told the judge that he didn't want to "walk down the same path as his father." Nevertheless, he received 42 months in federal lockup and was ordered to forfeit $600,000 in drug profits.

Bruno Indelicato, who served as the driver on the Santoro murder, pleaded guilty to lesser charges and was sentenced to 20 years in prison. He is incarcerated in the federal lockup at Fort Dix, New Jersey. He won't be released until 2023, when he will be 76 years old.

Bruno had worried that his father-in-law Jimmy Burke wouldn't come out of prison alive. Now, he too, may very well die behind bars.

Dominick wondered if Bruno really ever liked Burke. "Actually, I don't even know if Bruno even likes himself when he looks in the mirror. He had to be around Joe Massino and the other people who murdered his father and he didn't do anything about it. How could he hold his head high? They call me a rat, but is what he did really any better? Bruno needed an excuse for letting Joe Massino off the hook for killing his father. So he told people that John Gotti said that Massino had nothing to do with it. But why was John Gotti's word worth anything?"

Not that Dominick had a personal beef with Gotti. In fact, he said he admired Gotti's rise to the top of the Gambino family.

"I respected John," Dominick said. "He had the balls to make a move on Paul Castellano. But Gotti was a degenerate gambler who had a big mouth. He was too flashy. He acted like he was in Hollywood and he started believing his own press. He had charisma and he made himself so flamboyant that he destroyed this life. He turned it into a comedy show. That was the start of the downfall. This is supposed to be a secret life. But now, Gotti's grandsons have a TV show and the public knows all about the mob.

"Gotti was never boss material. He had an ego problem, which is why he made all his captains go once a week to his social club. He wanted to wield his power, but he was making it easy for the feds to identify the mob guys."

The Gambinos would have been better served with Salvatore "Sammy the Bull" Gravano as their boss, said Dominick. He explained that Gravano, who served as Gotti's underboss, knew the importance of staying off the FBI whiteboards.

"Gotti got caught throwing Sammy under the bus on federal tape recordings," Dominick said. "He blamed everything on Sammy. But if Sammy had been running things, the family would have been better off. Sammy and I both believed in keeping a low profile and being strategic about family business. He once told me, 'Vinny Basciano and John Gotti play checkers; we play chess.'"

When it comes to John Gotti Jr., however, Dominick has blunt criticism. "Junior rode his father's coattails. He was a steroid head. He'd go out with 15 guys and start problems. But I know he ratted to the government. He gave the feds information, just like I did. Whether you give the government a lot or a little, you're a rat. He talks a lot of phony shit on TV, but I don't see him living up to what he did. He has his mother and his sister telling the media that he's a victim. But he wasn't a victim when he killed people; he wasn't a victim when he took the oath of omerta. Junior says he's retired, but he's still in the life. He might be shelved right now (meaning he's inactive), but he's in the life. We never retire from this thing. This is not General Motors or IBM, where we could retire with a pension. Our retirement package is a bullet to the back of the head."

Dominick was called to testify against John Gotti Jr. in 2009. He said he didn't feel nervous about taking the stand against Junior. "I was more nervous about being confronted by his sister, Victoria," he said, explaining that he once had a brief relationship with her. "We had met at Rao's one night. She was out with a guy, but she slipped me her telephone number. I met her downtown. I was intrigued because, in a way, she was mob royalty."

CHAPTER 8
All Bets Are Off

Now 47, Dominick was released from prison in 2013, after serving eight years of a 10-year sentence for various mob-related crimes, including murder. He had originally faced two life terms for his involvement in the Pizzolo and Santoro killings. But Brooklyn Federal Judge Nicholas Garaufis reduced the sentence, citing Dominick's "extraordinary assistance" in helping the government dismantle the Bonanno leadership.

He said he's not afraid of possible retribution. "I'm living a different life now and minding my own business," he said. "I'm not in their backyard and they're not in mine. I choose not to run. But if I find out that someone is looking for me; if I catch them out of order, then all bets are off. I'm confident that I can handle whatever comes my way."

Recalling the winter night in 2001 at Rao's, Dominick said he sometimes misses the camaraderie of the guys, the money, and the power that came with the life.

"The Mafia is not just another criminal organization," he said. "It's an elite group in which you might have hardcore thugs who are basically buffoons, but you also have a lot of Mafioso who are very clever. Some of us were rubbing shoulders with bank presidents and politicians. For a street guy to be around people of influence, it's fascinating and impressive."

Saying the food at Rao's was "just okay—I never cared for their so-called famous meatballs," he admittedly enjoyed the intermingling of gangsters and celebrities.

"I once sat one table away from Bill Clinton," he mused. And there was the night when comedian Don Rickles looked at Vinny and Dominick and announced, "I better watch what I say; the Mafia is here." Rickles then attempted a creaky genuflection at their table.

"We laughed; it was in good humor," Dominick recalled. "We always blended in. We kept it low-key, never loud. The wiseguys from Brooklyn and Queens were noisy, with the pinky rings and the yelling Italian slang at each other. They'd go to clubs with 15 or 20 guys. But guys from the Bronx and Italian Harlem, like us, weren't showoffs. We had to be discreet because we were in big-money businesses. We didn't go out in a show of force and attract attention."

Contemplating Vinny's squandering of the Lufthansa heist money, Dominick, his one-time protégé and best friend, said, "It's hard to believe that he blew it senselessly on gambling. Personally, I would have invested it in real estate or construction. I would have looked to make more money with it, not piss it away at casinos."

But what about the $1 million in precious stones that has never been recovered?

Federal authorities suspect Burke gave the jewels to Vincent Asaro, who oversaw the Bonanno family's illicit activities at JFK airport. Asaro reportedly was supposed to have passed the jewels upwards as Burke's tribute to a high-ranking Bonanno, most likely Philip Rastelli or Joseph Massino. However, in a 2011 conversation recorded by the FBI, Asaro is heard complaining about Burke not sharing the loot.

"We never got our right money, what we were supposed to get, we got fucked all around," Asaro is heard telling an informant, who is thought to be Massino. "Got fucked all around. That fucking Jimmy [Burke] kept everything."

Some insiders say Burke stashed the jewels. Dominick believes that a portion of Burke's Lufthansa proceeds were used to finance the launch of Cathy Burke's jewelry store.

...Perhaps the Lufthansa jewels ended up there also?

SOURCE NOTES

In researching certain aspects of the crime and various mob figures, two books were referenced:

Vinny Gorgeous: The Ugly Rise and Fall of a New York Mobster, by Anthony DeStefano

The Sixth Family: The Collapse of the New York Mafia and the Rise of Vito Rizzuto, by Lee Lamothe and Adrian Humphreys

Several articles from the New York Daily News and The New York Times were also consulted

Robert Sberna

Printed in the USA
CPSIA information can be obtained
at www.ICGtesting.com
LVHW090825200824
788749LV00027B/130

9 780692 426807